To Molly

POCKET-BOOK SHAKESPEARE

Patricia Christie

Illustrated
by
Roger Eburne

love, Trish

ARTHUR H. STOCKWELL LTD
Torrs Park, Ilfracombe, Devon, EX34 8BA
Established 1898
www.ahstockwell.co.uk

First published in Great Britain, 2012

British Library Cataloguing-in-Publication Data.
A catalogue record for this book is available
from the British Library.

ISBN 978-0-7223-4219-0
Printed in Great Britain by
Arthur H. Stockwell Ltd
Torrs Park Ilfracombe
Devon EX34 8BA

For Joan and John

CONTENTS

FLIGHTS OF FANCY

"The mummers are here! The mummers are here!" The shout resounded through the marketplace.

A young boy, on his way to school, quickly turned round and followed the crowd to the green, where a travelling fair had been set up.

"This is too good to be missed," he said to himself. "I don't care if it means a beating when I get to school."

He sat cross-legged on the ground in front of the stage and watched the performance in wonder. How he longed to join the actors in their flights of fancy to other lands, to other ages – a battle here, a court scene there, a storm at sea! He marvelled at the antics of the comedians and was entranced by it all.

The church clock tolled the twelfth hour and he reluctantly left the green, pausing briefly to look at the fire-eater, the dancing bear, the cockfight and all the other attractions of the fair. By the time he got to school the scholars had reassembled after the break. His absence earned him a beating and a detention at the end of the school day.

On his way home he went down to the river – a favourite spot for his musings. Idly he threw sticks into the water and watched their progress. If only he had a boat and could travel to foreign lands! Perhaps he'd meet pirates on the way. Or else he'd be a brave sailor fighting for his country and good Queen Bess. Maybe he'd land on a desert island and wrestle with the natives; travel back in time to ancient Rome and be a gladiator; discover new countries with exotic beasts . . .

With a sigh he got up and wandered his way through the town. An inn with sounds of bawdy laughter coming forth was too much for his curiosity and he crept in under one of the tables.

"Wench! Bring us more ale," shouted one of the men.

A buxom female approached and the boy's eyes nearly started out of his head at the sight of her plump bosom.

"Ripe pomegranates, these," shouted a drunken oaf as he made a grab for her.

She boxed his ears and then glanced under the table.

"You young scamp!" she exclaimed. "Git out of 'ere." And with a sharp kick she propelled him into the street.

By the time he got home it was late. His mother shook her fist at him.

"Look at the state of your breeches," she shrieked. "Bed for you, my lad, and no supper!"

The next morning he took his usual route through the woods, imagining warlocks and witches behind every tree; wild beasts and hobgoblins round every bend in the path.

Another beating awaited his late arrival at the school. He was made to sit in the corner and transcribe vast tracts from the Bible.

The schoolmaster remonstrated with him: "If you don't attend to your lessons, you'll never get anywhere, Will Shakespeare."

THE COMEDY OF ERRORS

(Tune: 'Let's All Go to the Music Hall')

Let us all go to Ephesus where two sets of twins are in a fix.
Let us all go to Ephesus to witness such a muddle, such a mix.
The masters both are named the same, Antipholus;
The servants likewise both are Dromio,
So we're bound to see some fun before the hectic day is done.
Let's all go to Ephesus.

(Tune: 'I Do Like to Be Beside the Seaside')

When these two sets of twins were tiny babies
They set off to sail with Mum and Dad,
But a great big storm rose up and the family was split up –
One pair with Dad, one pair with Mum. Very sad!

(Tune: 'All the Nice Girls Love a Sailor')

So the master who lives in Ephesus and his servant out one day
Just don't appreciate that their twin brothers
Have come from Syracuse to stay.
Such a mix-up, such a muddle,
When no one ever knows who's who.
E'en the wife of one is fooled when her bro'-in-law she's pulled.
What to do? What to do?

(Tune: 'Daisy, Daisy')

Dad has come from Syracuse searching for wife and sons.
Mum has been in Ephesus living amongst the nuns.
The twins then all meet each other,
All pleased to find their brother.
It's really quite odd – four peas in a pod –
But it's all been a lot of fun.

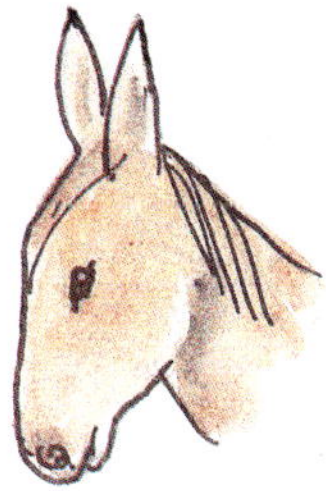

A MIDSUMMER NIGHT'S DREAM

There's a famous old play writ by Shakespeare
Which is called *A Midsummer Night's Dream*,
Where Oberon – a bit of a fairy –
Fell out with Titania, his queen.

"Hey oop!" said the King, all demanding.
"I want your pageboy just for me."
"Tough luck!" said Titania a-smirking.
"He is mine and my love, as you see."

And off she did flounce with her fairies
To the disco that raged in the dell.
"Just get on yer bike and go fer a hike,"
Titania so rudely did yell.

King Oberon, he weren't too happy.
"Come here, Puck," he did shout to his sprite.
"Make a potion from flowers and apply it
To the eyes of the Queen in the night.

"And then when she wakes in the morning
She'll love the first thing that she sees.
And I will make sure that it's shameful,
Which will bring her right down to her knees."

"Righto, boss," said young Puck as he flitted.
"I can whizz round the world in an hour.
In a jiff I'm a man, beast or maiden
And can find the appropriate flower."

Meanwhile, let us seek out the mortals
Where the Duke to his Hermia has said,
"You've got to marry Demetrius
And, if you don't, lass, you are dead."

"But, Father!" the girl said a-pleading.
"Lysander's the one I adore.
Don't make me be wife to D'metrius.
That very sad git is a bore."

She ran quickly off to her lover
And sobbed, "We're completely undone."
"We'll elope to the woods, my dear petal.
So take heart," said the son of a gun.

But Hermia told all to Helena
At a party when both were quite canned.
And Helen, who fancied Demetrius,
Told him what the two lovers planned.

So, off to the woods after midnight
The four of them stumbled around,
All trying to catch up with each other;
But they all fell asleep on the ground.

"Aha!" said the fairy king watching.
"These mortals are in such a stew.
Here, Puck, put some juice in the eyes
Of D'metrius, then see what he'll do.

"We'll get him to fall for Helena,
Which'll leave the two lovers alone."
"Pretty cool!" said young Puck. "I will soon
Make sure that I get the job done."

But Puck mistakes one man for t'other
And when young Lysander awakes,
He says, "Oh, Helena! I love you."
Says she, "Bugger off, you old fake."

So, Ob'ron gives juice to Demetrius
And he falls for Helena too.
She's pursued by them both and is angry
And shouts, "Help me! What shall I do?"

Meanwhile, in a glade in the forest
Some artisans practise a play,
Nick Bottom, a weaver, demanding,
"I'll be the lion on the day."

They all separate from each other
And Puck spies the weaver asleep.
"Aha! I'll transform his head to an ass,
Which'll make the confusion so deep."

Queen Titania, at last, is awakened
And shouts, "What a beautiful head!
I shall fondle your ears, my dear lover,
As you lie on my flowery bed."

Well, Bottom, of course, is delighted.
"I really don't mind if I do.
I like being pampered by fairies.
My pleasures, till now, have been few."

In the meantime, the unhappy mortals
All wander around in a mix
Till Oberon sorts out the problems,
And when they wake up all is fixed.

He also flits off to Titania.
"Wake up, dearest Queen," he did say.
She looks at the ass and says, "Heavens!
Why is this beast here, I pray?"

She makes it all up with her husband.
The fairies shout, "Hip hip hooray!"
The mortals get wed to their lovers
And they all settle down to the play.

As Pyramus, Bottom is champion.
The rest of the cast are a wow,
And Puck, the young scamp, whispers softly,
"What pranks can I get up to now?"

 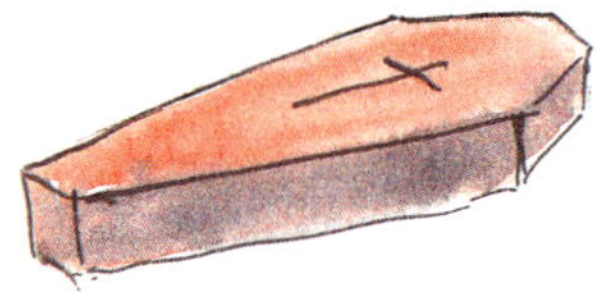

THE SEVEN SECRETS OF LIFE

'At first the infant, mewling and puking . . .'

"Where has this red hair come from?" muses the father as he looks at his son for the first time. "What is my wife not telling me?"

Then the schoolboy 'creeping like snail unwillingly to school. . . .'

Now that he knows that Santa Claus is not real he wonders what other secrets his parents have been keeping from him.

'Then the lover, sighing like furnace, with a woeful ballad . . .'

He spies a girl across a crowded room. She and her friends whisper and giggle together. How he'd love to break in on their confidences and whisk her away.

'Then a soldier, full of strange oaths . . . sudden and quick in quarrel . . .'

He finds the secrecy of being a member of the SAS too much for him and he plans a career change.

He becomes a lawyer 'with eyes severe, and beard of formal cut . . .'

He plays his part well and guards the confidential affairs of his clients with integrity.

‘The sixth age shifts into the lean and slipper’d pantaloon . . .’
The family treat him as a child and he accuses them of talking about him covertly in dark corners.

The ‘last scene of all . . . sans teeth, sans eyes, sans taste, sans everything. . . .’
This where the final secret of life is revealed: ‘mere oblivion’.

ROMEO AND JULIET

It was the afternoon of the big match – the traditional New Year derby between Rangers and Celtic. Glasgow fans converged, in their thousands, as they made their way towards Ibrox, many of them singing – still happily under the influence of too much indulgence from the previous evening. Ron and his pals, sporting their blue Rangers scarves, passed a couple of girls sitting on a wall.

"Hey!" said Ron. "See her? Thon Jules? She's hot stuff, so she is."

"Is thon the wee hairy you jived wi' at the Palais the ither nicht?"

"Aye. She's a braw wee lassie, thon. I don't half fancy her."

"Youse fancy a' the lassies, Ron. Ye're a right old Romeo, so ye are."

"Get lost, youse! She's a wee smasher, so she is. Nice legs too."

The good-natured banter continued as they made their way into the ground. The fans were strictly segregated by wire enclosures, as feelings amongst the crowd always ran high – no matter what the score.

After a nail-biting match the result was a 2–1 win for Celtic, with a disputed penalty goal the decider.

Outside the grounds the usual after-match fight took place. Ron and his mates joined in with gusto. At one point Ron found himself facing a bloke he knew from his schooldays.

"Tye!" he shouted. "Whit are youse doing supporting the left-footers? They're rubbish. Have to cheat to win, so they do."

"Youse take that back," said Tye, whipping out his flick knife. "An' anither thing: keep awa' frae my cousin, Jules. I heard you an' she wuz intae some heavy necking the ither nicht."

"Michty! Is she your cousin? I feel sorry fur her, so I do. Whit a family tae belong tae."

The two of them launched themselves at each other, but the police soon waded in and arrested them. A night in the cells and a stiff fine the next day sobered them up, but they both left the court vowing revenge.

The next Saturday, at the Palais, Ron claimed Jules for a smoochy dance to the latest Beatles number. She seemed subdued.

"Whit's the matter, hen?" he asked. "Ye're affy quiet."

"It's my dad. Thon sneaky Tye telt him aboot us. He says I hivna to hiv onything tae dae wi' ye."

"Whit wey not?"

"He says him an' your auld man fell oot, big time, in a gang fight in the Gorbals years ago."

"Whit's that got tae dae wi' us? We fancy each ither, don't we?"

"Aye."

"Tae hell wi' them. We'll dae oor ain thing. We could aye go tae Gretna Green an' mak' it legal. Whit do ye say tae that, hen?"

"Oh, jings, Ron! D'ye mean it?"

"Aye, I do. We'll ging the nicht, lassie, an' bugger the lot o' them."

The young lovebirds clutched each other while they danced

and whispered plans on how to make their getaway later that night. They parted outside the dance hall and went their separate ways.

At midnight Ron approached Jules' house.

"Crivvens! Whit's thon light daein' in yon window?" he muttered to himself.

He threw up a pebble to hit the glass and hid behind a tree. The light went out and the window opened.

"Ron, Ron, whaur are ye, Ron?" whispered Jules.

"I'm here, hen – doon in the street. Can ye sneak oot the hoose?"

"Aye, I'll be wi' ye in a minute."

The two youngsters were soon speeding away on Ron's motorbike. Jules clutched him as they went through the darkened streets.

"Are we really goin' tae Gretna?" she shouted.

"Aye, whit wey no? We hiv tae pit in fifteen days staying somewhere afore we get hitched, so it might as well be there."

"Whit a romantic ye are!"

Jules smiled and clung on as they left the outskirts of Glasgow. Ron revved up the bike and headed south. He had brought a tent, so once they'd found a campsite they settled down for the compulsory wait.

One day, when they returned from a trip out on the bike, they found Tye standing by the tent.

"Whit are ye daein' here?" demanded Jules.

"Whit dae ye think?" he replied. "I've come tae tak' ye hame, ye slut."

"Oh, no, ye winna," said Ron. "We wuz mairrit yesterday, so ye canna dae onything aboot it. And don't ye dare ca' my wife a slut."

He launched himself at Tye and punched him on the nose. The two went for each other, rolling over on the ground with Jules desperately trying to separate them. The flick knives came out and the fighting continued until Tye gave a moan of anguish. Ron staggered to his feet, his knife dripping blood.

"Oh, my Gawd! Whit hiv I done?" The two stood looking with horror at Tye as the breath left his body.

"Jings, Ron, we'd better get awa' frae here quick, afore someone calls the polis."

"It's nae your fault, hen. You stay. I'll ging aff on my own."

"I'm comin' wi' ye, so forget it. Till death dae wiz part, remember?"

They scrambled on to the bike and quickly sped out of the site, heading south of the Border.

The next day the local newspaper reported that a young couple had been killed when their motorbike collided with a lorry on the A74. The bodies had been recovered from the verge, clutched in an embrace.

THE MERCHANT OF VENICE

The Merchant of Venice – a Jew –
Was hated by most folks he knew.
When he lent out his cash
He charged interest so rash
That borr'wers were left feeling blue.

One day he met An-toni-o
Who, of all, was his deadliest foe.
Tony wanted some money.
The Jew said, "That's funny!
There are several rules you should know:

"If the forfeit you cannot repay
By a certain time, then, come what may,
I might have a bash
At removing some flesh
From your chest – just for fun. What d'you say?"

Tone agreed, but soon news on his phone
Revealed he could not pay his loan.
Shylock whipped out his knife,
Hoped to end his foe's life,
While Antonio let out a moan.

The Judge, a young girl in disguise,
Looked at Shylock – right into his eyes.
"Pound of flesh, now, no more –
No bone, blood or gore –
Or you are the one here who dies."

Poor old Shylock! It's always the same:
He's ridiculed – covered with shame.
Nothing left he can pawn.
All his ducats are gone
And he ends up with nowt to his name.

THE MERRY WIVES

(A Pantomime)

Characters: Anne Page
Mistress Page
Person
Mistress Ford
Falstaff
Fenton

ANNE: Alas, alack! My name is Anne, tho' Father calls me Annie.
He says I have to wed his chum and get up off my— backside.
O, woe is me! What shall I do? I'm nagged at by my mother.
She says she's found a man for me, but I – I love another.

ENTER MISTRESS PAGE, A MAN IN DRAG.

MISTRESS PAGE: Hello, my love. Ignore your dad. The suitor that I've found
Will be the very chap for you. He's French, but awfully sound.

ANNE: But, Mum, I love dear Fenton.

MISTRESS PAGE: Oh, no, you don't.

ANNE: I do.

MISTRESS PAGE: Oh, no, you don't, my darling girl. He's not the lad for you.
Now, off you go and clean the pots and sweep the floors and mats.
My dear friend, Mistress Ford is due for one of our wee chats.

EXIT ANNE. ENTER A PERSON DRESSED AS ALADDIN FOLLOWED BY MISTRESS FORD (MAN IN DRAG) TEXTING ON MOBILE.

PERSON: I'd love to do a pantomime; Aladdin is my name.
I've come from far off Chinatown to seek fortune and fame.

MISTRESS FORD: You've got it wrong, you silly chap. It's *Merry Wives* on stage.
Go find another pantomime. Leave me with Mistress Page.

EXIT PERSON IN A HUFF.

MISTRESS FORD: And now, my dear, guess what I've had – a text from that old sinner.
From Falstaff – wants to make a date, tonight before his dinner.

MISTRESS PAGE: Well, what a cheek! He's e-mailed me. [*READING*] He says, 'Dear Mistress Page,
I know you really fancy me as I am all the rage.'

MISTRESS FORD: Let's hatch a plot to bring him down. Let's really make him suffer.

MISTRESS PAGE: Behind you – look!

MISTRESS FORD: Behind me, what?

MISTRESS PAGE: Behind you – that old duffer.

ENTER FALSTAFF WITH iPOD. EXEUNT DAMES

FALSTAFF: I dig this song. It makes me hot and up for any games
With Mistress Ford and Mistress Page – those luscious sexy dames.

ENTER PERSON DRESSED AS PRINCE CHARMING.

PERSON: Prince Charming! That is who I'll be – a dashing handsome fella.
I'll search the land! I'll find my love! I'll marry Cinderella!

FALSTAFF: Get lost, you cheeky, saucy fool! I am the one who's best
At pulling all the chicks round here. So scarper off, you pest.

PERSON EXITS TO HISSING AND BOOING. ENTER MISTRESS FORD WITH LARGE LAUNDRY BASKET.

FALSTAFF: Well, hi, my dear. At last you've come. So, how's about a grope?

MISTRESS FORD: Oh, no, you don't!

FALSTAFF: Oh, yes, I do.

MISTRESS FORD: Oh, no, you don't, you dope.
Behind you – look!

FALSTAFF: Behind me, where?

MISTRESS FORD: Behind you comes my friend.

ENTER MISTRESS PAGE.

FALSTAFF: What shall I do? Where shall I hide?
MISTRESS FORD: Climb in – a hand I'll lend.

FALSTAFF CLIMBS INTO BASKET.

MISTRESS PAGE: The stupid fool has fallen for our plan – worked like a dream.
We'll get our servants on the job to throw him in the stream.

EXEUNT, PUSHING BASKET. ENTER ANNE AND FENTON.

ANNE: Alas, alack! O, woe is me! My parents ban our love.
O, Fenton, we are doomed, I fear.
FENTON: Don't worry, my dear dove.
Tonight, at midnight, in the woods when fairy frolics flutter
I'll whisk you off, make you my wife, then nothing else will matter.

EXEUNT. MIDNIGHT STRIKES. ENTER MISTRESS PAGE AND MISTRESS FORD, LAUGHING.

MISTRESS PAGE: What merry japes we've played tonight. We've rumbled that old git.
By luring Falstaff to the woods we've got him in the— manure!

MISTRESS FORD: Those kids were great dressed up as elves. They made a fearsome sight
When prancing round old Falstaff, who screamed with all his might.

MISTRESS PAGE AND MISTRESS FORD HIGH-FIVE EACH OTHER.

BOTH: [*SINGING*] There is nothing like a dame!

ENTER ANNE AND FENTON.

ANNE: Hi, Mum! I'm Mrs F.

MISTRESS PAGE: Oh, no!

ANNE: I am.

MISTRESS PAGE: Oh, no, you're not.

ANNE: I'm married now. The play is done. It's over. That's your lot!

ENTER PERSON DRESSED AS DR WHO.

PERSON: At last they all have finished. It's time to play my part.
They've signed me up as Dr Who – a new career to start.

THE END

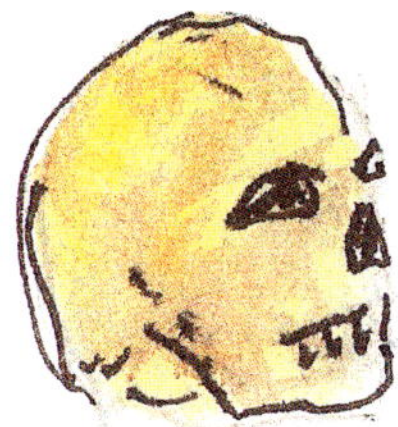

HAMLET

(Tune: 'My Old Man Said Follow the Van')

My old man was king of the realm,
And now he's nothing but a ghost.
Wand'ring around on the roof of the castle,
Hoping his death is avenged with hassle.
So I pondered and wondered, wondered and pondered,
Lost my reason, gave a mighty moan
When Ma in unseemly haste got wed to my uncle,
Who now sits on Father's throne.

(Tune: 'Tea for Two')

To be or not
To be. I see
This deadly plot
Is up to me.
I'll see if I can find a way to sleep,
Perchance to dream. It may well seem that death is not the end.
It's been a living nightmare here in Elsinore.

(Tune: 'Waiting at the Church')

There was she hopeful by the church,
Hopeful by the church, hopeful by the church.
Poor Ophelia, he left her in the lurch.
Lord, how it did upset her!
All at once she took a little dip,
A wet and deadly trip, with garlands on her hip.
Hamlet was mad, went out and killed her dad.
Bodies a-ccru-ing.

(Tune: 'After the Ball')

After the play was over, after they'd seen the mime,
After the poisoned liquid revealed that there'd been a crime,
Uncle was looking guilty, Mother was anguished too.
Hamlet was banished to foreign parts, but he'd more work to do.

(Tune: 'Bull and Bush')

Come, come, see Hamlet fighting
For now he is back from his cruise.
Come, come, watch Mum and Uncle
Drink poison that's poured in the booze.
See how many bodies fly – ta-ra-ra-ra-ra-ra-ra!
Hamlet and all his mates die.
Don't, don't have a drink at Elsinore. No one is left there to cry.

MACBETH

My wife made me do it. She's always been ambitious – for money, position, power. Talk about keeping up with the Joneses! She'd do anything to get what she wants, but when murder was suggested I dug my heels in.

"No way!" I said. "Can't be done. Anyway, old Len will die sooner or later and then I'll be the boss."

"No guarantee of that," she replied. "He might decide that Scottish git, Jock, should be the one in charge. Then where would you be?"

"Well, I draw the line at murder."

"Come on! Don't be such a wimp. I've thought of a foolproof plan."

"No such thing," I muttered. "We're bound to be found out."

But on and on she went. You know how women can grind you into the dust with their constant nagging? Well, that's my wife. She just doesn't let up once she's got her teeth into something. Eventually (just to shut her up, you understand) I gave in and listened to her plan.

"When you and Len come out of the pub on Saturday night, mingle with some yobs and pick a fight, you can easily knock them out. Then knife Len, drag him to the car and bring him back here to phone for help. We can always finish him off before the ambulance arrives, if he isn't dead already."

"Bloody hell! It'll never work! What if the yobs do me in first?"

"Never – what with your army training and judo black belt! You can do it."

"Get lost, woman!"

Days went by and the nagging continued. It did my head in. And then one Friday, at work, Len said he wanted a management meeting for the following week. He said he was planning to restructure the business and how it was run. I managed to sneak a look at his computer when he was out of his office and, sure enough, the wife was right. Jock appeared to be next in line when Len retired. I boiled with anger. After all the years I had put in and the flack I'd had to take, that pipsqueak, young Jock, was to be the boss!

When I got home and told the wife, she exploded: "What did I tell you? You'll be out of a job in no time with that grease pot in charge. Now will you consider my plan?"

'Hmm, maybe. But—"

"No buts. If you're going to do it, do it now while you're good and angry."

"OK – tomorrow I'll give it a go if it's at all possible."

And I did. It was amazingly easy. When Len and I came out of the pub there were actually a couple of hoodies hanging round my car. I grabbed them both and knocked their heads together; then I knifed Len and shoved him in the car. There was no one else around, so I knelt down beside one of the half-senseless yobs, smeared him with blood and stuffed the knife into his hand.

When I reached home, the wife and I carried Len into the house and dumped him on the sofa.

While she phoned for an ambulance I finished the poor old bugger off with the same kind of knife I'd used earlier and cut myself in a few places to make it look like we had both been attacked.

"Ugh, what a lot of blood!" my wife said as she removed the knife. "Give me your gloves as well and I'll wash the lot before I bury them in the garden."

She'd worked it all out. What a woman!

The ambulance and police arrived at the same time. Photos and statements were taken, questions asked. Why had I brought him back to the house instead of calling an ambulance on the spot? My reply was that I didn't realise how badly hurt he was and I had no mobile on me. The wife did a great act as the hysterical woman who had lost a dear friend. The body was removed. Patrol cars were alerted to search for the two yobs. And eventually the police left, promising to return the next day.

That night neither of us slept well. In my head I went over and over my story to the police so that it would be firmly lodged. The wife – would you believe it? – was in a right old state, getting more nervous by the minute. She was up and down to the loo all night long, wandering around the room, wringing her hands.

"All that blood!" she said. "What if the fuzz don't believe us? What if . . . ?"

"Listen, you stupid cow: it was all your idea, remember? Foolproof, you said. So shut up and go to sleep. Just stick to the story and we'll be OK."

The next morning I told her to keep mum and let me do the talking when the cops came. The police had found the crime scene with blood on the ground and a knife thrown in the hedge, but had not caught up with the youths. After many more questions I agreed to go with the cops to the scene. I was feeling confident by then that we'd get away with it.

At work on the Monday an appalled management team met in Len's office. I repeated my version of the event and made light of my injuries. When I produced my doctored memo of Len's plans for the future, it showed me as the person in charge. There was a shocked silence and one or two people glanced at Jock.

"I think, as a mark of respect for Len, we should close down till after the funeral," I suggested, "but perhaps we could all meet here in a week's time?"

Jock looked at me suspiciously as they filed solemnly out of the room.

"I'll get you for this, Mac," he said. "See if I don't, you murdering bastard!"

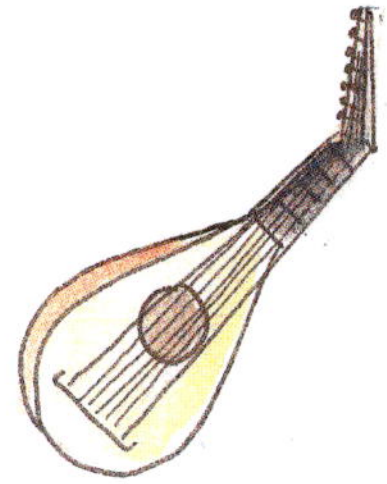

MUCH ADO ABOUT NOTHING

Much Ado About Nothing's a grand play
'Bout jealousy, passion and love,
Where our Beatrice and Benedick quarrel
But unite whene'er push comes to shove.

It begins with Don John and Don Pedro,
When they go to Le'nato's to stay
With Claudio, Benedick and others.
It ends up a jolly part – ay!

The daughter of Le'nato is Hero –
A beautiful lass all agree –
And her cousin, the intrepid Beatrice,
Has a tongue that's as sharp as can be.

When she meets up with handsome young Ben'dick
They each score points one off the other.
Sparks fly as they fight, but both are content
And deny that they wish for a lover.

But Claudio when he sees young Hero
Is smitten with love through and through.
She fancies him rotten, but is very shy.
They neither know what they should do.

To Don Pedro does Claudio whisper
And asks him his Hero to woo.
At the ball, where she's masked, there she is asked
If she'd like to say "Yes" and "I do".

Don John, who's a bit of a bastard,
Hates Claude and decides to cause strife
When he overhears plans of the nuptials.
He'll stop them from being man and wife.

Meanwhile back to our Be'trice and Ben'dick
(To be easy, let's say B and B):
They've been tricked by their friends who have noticed
That they both from their true feelings flee;

That they each like to hide their emotions;
That true love really is very blind;
That their fighting is just a defence
From what act'ly goes on in the mind.

And now to Don John's machinations,
Where a stand-in for Hero tricks Claude
As she makes violent love to another,
So he thinks it's his love's love that's flawed.

Well, the groom is so shattered he reckons
He'll wait till the wedding day's there.
He declares that his bride is a harlot
And she faints at his feet in despair.

Leonato and B and B protest
That their Hero is chaste through and through.
But Claude rushes off in a passion,
So the priest tells them what they should do.

"Pretend Hero's dead," says the pastor,
"Then Claudio will feel much remorse."
B and B, left alone, are so tongue-tied,
But, at last, confess love's a strong force.

"I'll do anything," says a rash Ben'dick
As he tries to calm Beatrice's rage.
"Kill Claudio," she says, "as proof of your love,
Or for ever on you war I'll wage."

Off goes the poor man to seek Claudio,
But he meets with t'night watch on the way
Who'd spied on Don John's evil plotting,
So he soon for his crime had to pay.

To atone contrite Claude says he'll marry
A lookalike Hero who's masked
At an action replay of the wedding.
And the lady says, "I do," when asked.

Of course, it's his true love, and Claudio
Says, "Sorry! Let's make up in bed."
And B and B look at each other
And very soon they are both wed.

The moral of this tale for lovers:
That if you with rumours are hit
Beware of false whispers from others,
Or you'll end up for ever in— trouble!

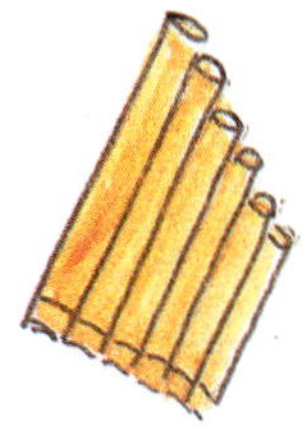

THE TAMING OF THE SHREW

From: info@lucentio.edu.padua
To: signorbaptista@interview.com
Subject: Job Application

Dear Signor Baptista,

I wish to apply for the post of tutor to your daughter, Bianca. My CV and references can be viewed on my website – www.lucentio.edu.padua

Yours sincerely,

Signor Lucentio

From: bianca@tesco.co.it
To: info@lucentio.edu.padua
Subject: Ghastly Sister

Bravo, Lucentio! How clever of you to disguise yourself as my tutor! But my father will never consent to our marriage. He already has two suitors lined up – an old fart and a teenage yob. Anyway, he refuses to allow me to become engaged until my elder sister, Katherina, is married. She is a right old bitch with a shrewish temper who scares everyone away. No one will want her as a wife. I'll end up on the shelf because of her.

Yours in despair,

Bianca

From: info@lucentio.edu.padua
To: petruchio@gigglemail.com
Subject: Katherina Baptista

Dear Friend,

I heard on the grapevine that you are looking for a wife. I have found just the one for you. Meet me at the pub tonight.

Regards,

Lucentio

From: katherina@sodoff.co.it
To: petruchio@gigglemail.com
Subject: Marriage

Get lost, you useless git! If you think I'd look twice at you or any other bloke in this godforsaken town, you must be madder than you look. Bugger off!

Kate B.

From: petruchio@gigglemail.com
To: katherina@sodoff.co.it
Subject: Wooing

My darling, sweet Kate,

How I love it when you speak to me in those dulcet tones. Your eyes – flashing with desire – melt my racing heart. When you throw things at me I just know how much you want me to wed you and bed you. By the way, the marriage takes place tomorrow. Pack for a long journey.

Your ever devoted
Petruchio

From: katherina@sodoff.co.it
To: bianca@tesco.co.it
Subject: Mad Husband

Sister,

I have married an idiot. He turns up at our wedding dressed like a clown, drags me straight afterwards on a tedious journey in a ramshackle vehicle to his shambolic house, starves me, keeps me awake all night and refuses me new clothes – all the while professing he loves me. The man is mad! We are coming back for your wedding next week. I'll be the one in rags, having a bad hair day.

Kate

From: petruchio@gigglemail.com
To: info@lucentio.edu.padua
Subject: Taming the Shrew

My dear friend,

I wish you well with your bride, Bianca – a splendid girl, but not a patch on my meek and gentle Kate. As she demonstrated at your wedding, she was the only wife to obey her husband's command. I am truly blessed.

Yours smugly,

Petruchio

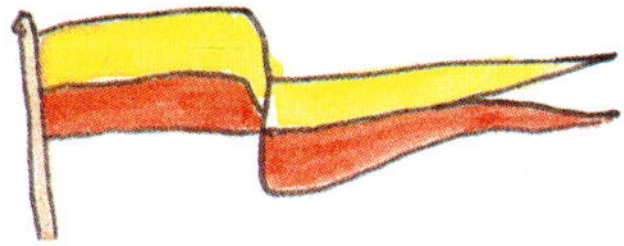

LET'S FALL IN LOVE

You do it; we do it; characters in many Shakespeare plays do it
– Let's do it, let's fall in love.

Cleopatra with a snake does it;
Cassius when he's on the make does it –
Let's do it, let's fall in love.

In her sleep Lady Macbeth does it at considerable length;
King Hal at Agincourt does it with remarkable strength.

Othello believing tales does it;
Prospero almost drowned in gales does it –
Let's do it, let's fall in love.

Richard with his hump does it as he looks for a horse;
Brutus stabbing Caesar does it when he uses brute force.

King Lear poking eyes does it;
Duke Orsino with his lovelorn sighs does it –
Let's do it, let's fall in love.

Malvolio writing letters does it when his garters are crossed;
King John fighting wars does it, though the battle is lost.

Two Verona gents do it;
Henry Fourth's army in their tents do it –
Let's do it, let's fall in love.

Let's admit it folks, you do it; we do it;
Actors everywhere because it's free do it –
Let's do it, let's all fall in love.